My Father's Table

Denise Mercer Blackwell

Cover Photo: Williams' Friendly Family Restaurant,
               "Where Friends Meet, Greet & Eat"
               Statesville, NC

ISBN: 978-0991072101
ISBN: 0991072103

Printed in the United States of America
KAM Publishing

Table of Contents

Dedication

I dedicate this book to the honor and memory of my father. Dad's love, guidance, patience, understanding, and compassion spilled over from his life into the lives of others, an amazing gift and talent that allowed him to receive the benefits of watching the world around him grow. Dad was like water, and all who crossed his path were seeds thirsting to be "Mercerized," a far different, far more satisfying quenching than anything the world has to offer. Dad's water was served with kindness, humility, compassion, love, and respect. He taught us not to judge others, but to realize that everyone is doing the best they can at the moment.

That last year we spent together was filled with trips. We made memories I will forever cherish in my heart. We taught and shared about true life, and I came to understand that Dad and I were both blessed with the same gift. I loved how we exchanged smiles when, as if we had signs over our heads, the waitress we'd just met felt compelled and comfortable to share all of her troubles, struggles, and deepest, darkest secrets. I reveled in the fact that we could mutually offer that young woman the light we always carried inside. I was trained by the best earthly example, and although I will miss him, I know I am ready to carry Dad's torch. I long to do what Dad did while he was with us, to try to make the world a better place and serve anyone who crosses my path.

I will be forever grateful to my dad for sharing with me and helping me to grow in faith, especially during his last years. His memory will live on not only in me, but also in everyone who had the honor to find themselves in his path or at his table.

I also dedicate this work to my beloved grandmother. Grandma Lois, your guidance has been passed on through the Mercers. You are humble, kind, understanding, praising, and encouraging. The look that comes over your beautiful, wise face when you do not agree with my thoughts or decisions is priceless. Without a word, you let me know when I need to rethink an idea or an opinion, and you are almost always right! You were born in 1910, decades ago, and you are still making a difference in my life and the lives of my four children. Years ago, I gave you two boxes for Christmas, Grandma. Those boxes contained nothing elaborate—just simple, inexpensive angels for you to display in your home. Before you opened those trinkets, you said, "One box is more than enough." Perhaps you were right, for I know that you are one package that continues to deliver each day. I still have a simple index card you wrote and eventually passed on to me, a treasure of wisdom and frequent reminder: "Grace is giving to you what you don't deserve. Mercy is withholding that which you do deserve."

Grandma, at my wedding, you surprised me, and I surprised you at your 100th birthday celebration. I treasure in my heart the memories we've made together over the years, especially when you took me to buy Christmas presents for my mom, dad, and brothers and to pick out my pumpkin at the orchard. Distance has never separated our hearts. In fact, nothing ever will.

Bobby and Kelly, I had no idea that when we met, God had sent someone I truly needed into my life. You two have never given up on me, even when my days were dark and down. Thank you for standing by me and always encouraging me to take the next steps on my journey. Thank you for allowing me the time I needed to grow in several areas and in the ways that worked best for me, despite how difficult and painful it was to watch me stumble. Even when fear paralyzed me, you were there. You cared enough to learn my weaknesses, along with my strengths, and you paid attention to my signals so quick intervention could be exercised. You chose your words kindly and lifted me up rather than tearing me down. Thank you both for seeing the light and for walking with me along the journey. I am so blessed to share this life with both of you because you see the larger purpose in this world.

To RS, I know you have been sent into my life so that I may continue to gather around the table and devour more wisdom. I first visited the Coffee House in search of a quiet place to write, but more often these days, I cross that threshold just to hear your perspective, to laugh with you, and to leave you speechless. In such a short amount of time, you have made a huge impact on me, and I know God uses you often, whether you know it or not, to deliver His important messages to me. I believe one of a little girl's darkest days is the day she loses her daddy, no matter how old she is, and although no one can ever replace him, so often your words and actions make me feel like I am once again sharing his table. For that and so many other reasons, I am grateful to have met you.

To my readers, remember that you are special, unique, and good enough just the way you are. Sure, you may need to do some tweaking but you are good enough— maybe far better than you think. My sincere wish is that you will find something in these pages that will propel you to take your next step, a step in the right direction. I hope the words contained within these pages will cause you to think in a new way, to look at things from a new perspective. I want you to be inspired to begin or continue your journey, so that you may find not only a mediocre existence, but a life worth living. I don't want you to just make it or simply eke by. I want you to be passionate about living, and I sincerely hope this book will encourage you to do just that.

I haven't always known, understood, or lived life with the faith I have today. I was not raised in church, and to this day, I have very little knowledge of the Bible. At the ripe old age of 21, I moved over 700 miles away from home in search of two things. First, I wanted to bask in some warmer weather and second—and perhaps most importantly—I wanted to find out for myself if God is real. I do not boast of the blessings in my life because someone told me to believe. Rather, I boast because He has personally revealed to me His amazing grace and mercy each day. I encourage you to search, to seek Him out for yourself by taking one step at a time. If you make the journey, you will find your Higher Power, just as I did, and it may be the most freeing moment of your life. The faith of a mustard seed can move mountains. Our God is one of abundance, and He only wants the best for his children. If you are not living well, it cannot be blamed on God. Follow what God lays on your heart and take it one step at a time, allowing Him to guide you all the way. Trust the many promises He has given to us and live those promises daily.

You cannot show the light to others if your life is dark. If your actions, words, and faith do not exhibit the promises of God's Word, you will not win anyone over to your way of thinking. We cannot be hypocrites, telling others what they need to do and spouting off scriptures at them if we are not willing to take our own advice and heed the Bible ourselves. Choose your words carefully, for what you say and do will come back to you. Do not judge others just because their sins are different from yours. Everyone has their own journey to walk, and along the way, we are commanded to love our neighbors and our enemies.

Finally, and perhaps most of all, I must dedicate this book to my amazing God, the One who carries me through my trials and loves me through it all. The miracles He has allowed my family and me to take part in are simply incredible. May I continue to be a light to the world, always striving to become a beacon of His love and deliverance.

Jabez cried out to the God of Israel,"Oh, that you would bless me and enlarge my territory! Let your hand be with me, and keep me from harm so that I will be free from pain." And God granted his request.

I Chronicles 4:10 (NIV)

Introduction

"God does not make clones. Each person is different, a tribute to God's creativity. If we are to love our neighbors as ourselves, we must accept people as they are and not demand that they conform to our own image."

~ Henry Fehren

Karl Alan Mercer was born on July 7, 1945, the fourth child to Dale and Lois Mercer. A hardworking lad, he began working for his dad and paying into the Social Security system at only ten years old.

Karl's mother, Lois, had big dreams for her son and hoped he would grow up to become a lawyer or a doctor. Unfortunately, he could not meet the English requirements in college, so that dream did not become a reality. When Karl was nineteen, he was hired by General Motors. Lois was devastated at first, thinking her beloved son would have no chance at a bright future, but she grew to appreciate the employment opportunity General Motors had given him. Karl seemed satisfied and enjoyed the work, and that was all that mattered to his mother, who loved him very much.

When Karl was only twenty-four, his father, Dale was hit by a drunk driver and killed. The young man was asked to identify his father's body, collect his belongings, and break the grim news to his mother and three brothers, which would prove to be a heart-wrenching task.

Tragedy did not end there for young Karl, for less than a year later, his wife left him, forcing him to share custody of their young child. His life felt as if it was spiraling out of control, and he quickly turned to the bottle seeking an escape from reality. In time, Karl remarried and fathered two more children, but he continued to drink.

Before long, always seeking escape from pain that had settled deep in his core, Karl was both a workaholic and an alcoholic, and he began to base the quality of his life on how much money was in his pocket. Besides his full-time job as a pipefitter at GM, he worked many jobs on the side, including snow removal, driving a dump truck, running a wrecker service, and even volunteering as a firefighter and a pit crew member for his racing friends at the local racetracks. He also became a master plumber, and he owned and operated his own business for many years.

Karl, my father, struggled with accepting himself. He felt he was never good enough, no matter how hard he tried and how hard he worked. As a child, another boy had told him he couldn't play with the other kids simply because his jacket only bore one stripe, while the "cool" ones had two. He was good at his job at General Motors, but he blamed himself for years for failing at his college education. He was very intelligent, but he hadn't finished college, and that had always made him feel a little less than. He had not become a doctor, a lawyer, or a college graduate and that bothered him. Ironically, in his final years on Earth, his closest friends included a lawyer, a dentist, and a banker.

In spite of his troubles and the battles raging within him, my dad was always a goodhearted man who did his best to treat others with respect. He knew his drinking was a problem, and he wanted something different. He also realized he had no answers for life, and he was tired of living that way. Thus, he opened himself up to getting better, and he was willing to do anything the folks at Alcoholics Anonymous told him to do in order to bring about the changes he so desperately wanted but could not accomplish by himself.

Dad once told me the story of his first drink, and he remembered it vividly. While babysitting his niece, at the age of twelve, he became curious about a bottle of scotch and decided to take a drink. As he looked back on that pivotal moment in his life, he realized it should have been a red flag for him, a warning that he was, truly, an alcoholic; he finished nearly the entire pint, leaving only one gulp in the bottom of the bottle.

My father was never really concerned about the meeting of alcoholics being so anonymous, at least for him. He didn't care if people knew who he was or that he was a member of AA, but he wouldn't dare break anyone else's anonymity. He honored and respected the AA, and his actions proved that; Dad attended AA meetings seven days a week for nearly twenty-five years, and he really worked the Twelve Steps. He put real effort into each step and stayed in continuous contact with those steps, growing, tweaking, and digging deeper within himself. He even attended the meetings while on vacation or when company was visiting. Big events and social get-togethers made him cling to AA all the more, as those were the most difficult times to stay focused and "on the wagon." For Dad, AA was his lifeline. He was asked after many years of sobriety,

"Why do you still call yourself an alcoholic?" He responded to that question, "The day I forget who I am is the day I will be that person again." My dad always remained humble and shared his story with anyone who would listen. He hoped talking about his problem might help someone else overcome obstacles in their life, and his willingness to talk about it also helped him keep in mind who he was. By giving of himself, he was able to remain sober. Through that transformation, he also discovered that real joy in life can only be achieved when we are in service to others. Setting himself aside so he could focus on others brought so much to his life. When talking of my father, my grandma shared the following statement: "Doing for others makes life worthwhile."

Eventually, Dad reached a huge turning point in his life, and he was confronted with a question many of those on the brink of retirement have to ask themselves: What does a workaholic do with so much spare time? He had worked extra years to save up for retirement; he simply hadn't been ready to leave his employer, where he had the most seniority, had built relationships, and had earned a good paycheck, and he had no intention of having to work part-time in his golden years just to make ends meet. Still, financial concerns aside, retirement was difficult for him at first, especially since he moved 750 miles away from the life he'd built. Previously, he could do math nearly at the same speed as a calculator, but now he could no longer put two and two together—literally. My father's identity had always been quite linked to his job, and for the first time in almost fifty years, he was without one. He had to dig deep within himself, to take a long, hard look in the mirror, in order to evaluate what was really important. Dad had to find a new identity that was not connected to his former employment. It took a while, but he began making his mark on this new area that he now called home. He became heavily involved with AA service work because he believed in the amazing impact it could have on one's life, something he'd experienced for himself.

Dad continued to be others-focused, and before long an opportunity opened to become a Stephen Minister, a training program that would allow him to gain more skills and become more effective at helping others.

Just like most everyone he dealt with, he understood me better than I understood myself. He knew how to steer anyone without them even knowing they were being steered. Dad had a way of knowing all the unspoken things that were boiling beneath the surface. He knew when to give praise and when to be stern.

During Dad's final month of life, he had several visitors. One day when I walked into his room, there was a man there, speaking to him.

"Karl," the man said, "I need to go. I'm sorry. I came to lift you up, but as usual, you helped me."

I knew what he meant, as I had experienced the same thing. My dad was the sick one, but when people came to encourage him, he had the rare ability to get them to open up within minutes. Whatever the secret burden, he could unwrap it in just moments. Although his visitor felt guilty about that, I knew his visit had given my dad exactly what he needed: He'd allowed my dad to make a difference in the life of another.

Another man was someone I actually knew. He walked in the room and said, "I just came to get Mercerized."

My dad laughed and smiled humbly at him. He thought nothing of what he did by sharing with others, but he did come to understand that his words, kindness, and humility were making a positive impact. He learned that if he focused on others and not himself, he, as well as they, would feel better.

Dad wasn't one for traveling, but he took a vacation every time he gathered around a table. He learned to live each day as a vacation, seizing every opportunity. Sometimes he sat alone, but most of the time he dined with others, be it family, a waitress, a busboy, a complete stranger, or friends. No matter the situation, Dad found someone to talk to about life, passing tidbits of great information to anyone who would listen. Around the tables he listened, counseled, and passed on everything he had within him, helping others by just being himself.

There came a point when we both recognized our growing faith and our mutual gift of connecting with people, and he began teaching me deeper lessons. I even taught him a little along the way. We discussed many scenarios, problems, when we enjoyed meals together, and he taught me more about understanding people. I was his apprentice, and we both understood that a torch was being passed along to the next generation.

The words in the following pages are the culmination of my father's important words, crucial life lessons that I and many others have learned around *My Father's Table*.

CHAPTER 1

Guiding Principle

"Anything in life that we don't accept will simply make trouble for us until we make peace with it."

~ Shakti Gawain

Successful people follow guiding principles to help them through life. They are aware that there are both good and rough times; to them this is not unfair, but it is simply a reality. Successful men and women are prepared to weather the storms of the sea by relying on their guiding principles for shelter. A person who is truly connected to their guiding principles, someone who will not waver from them, can pass them on to others without others even being fully aware of it.

I had no idea that the guiding principle my dad lived by was also guiding me subconsciously, but now I am thrilled that it was passed on to me, and I am even more thrilled to be able to pass it on to others without even being aware that the lesson is happening: "God, grant me the serenity to accept the things I cannot change, the courage to change the things I can, and the wisdom to know the difference."

> God, grant me the
>
> serenity to accept the things I cannot change,
>
> the courage to change the things I can,
>
> and the wisdom to know the difference.

This principle is easy to memorize, and I am certain you have seen it in many places; however, I want you to truly internalize it for all it is worth. The words are simple yet so valuable, as the outcome of letting this principle guide you is serenity, the state or quality of being serene, calm, or tranquil.

For those of you who are not believers, you can take some solace in the fact that my father learned to live by this principle long before he had complete understanding of his faith. Before I had faith, I abided by this as well. If you don't know where your feelings truly lie about the existence or involvement of a Higher Power, I still believe you can agree with this life-altering creed.

Accept the Things You Cannot Change

Let me ask you a question: Do you really accept the things you cannot change, or is this just a great idea that seems more possible and fit for others? It is most definitely easier said than done, and it takes practice, effort, and a dedicated choice to live your life in this way.

Many things happen to us and around us in life, and while we'd like to think we have control over them, the truth is, we don't. Think about the following and how you would react. Are these changes you can accept?

- The power bill is higher than you expect, much higher than normal.

- The washing machine or another major appliance breaks.

- You receive frightening or unfavorable medical news.

- You encounter an accident, whether a car collision, a broken window, or spilled milk.

- You accidentally lock your keys in the car.

- Your spouse runs out of gas while on a trip.

- You face sudden termination of employment.

- There is a death of a loved one, expected or not.

When these sorts of things happen, when they are in the past, they cannot be undone; you cannot change them.

Do you dwell upon your past mistakes or the mistakes of others? Do you truly accept that there are some things you cannot change, or do you allow these things to control you? Is your head stuck on instant replay? Does your obsession over the past cripple your future?

This past Mother's Day, all four of my children were sitting on the bed beside me, getting ready to leave. My youngest daughter somehow took a dive off the bed and hit the side of her face on the bedside table. At the emergency room, the injury was treated with eight stitches. The situation made me sick to my stomach, as she was crying while they were trying to close the wound. On the way home, I replayed the incident over and over in my mind, beating myself up for being so close yet not being able to stop my child from being hurt. It did not take long for this guiding principle to pop into my head, and I switched to reciting to myself over and over, "Accept the things I cannot change. Accept the things I cannot change.

Accept the things I cannot change." I could have continued to beat myself up, to feel guilty and allow the incident to take up space in my mind, or I could accept that it had happened and move on to the next step, which was caring for her wound.

My oldest daughter, my father, and I traveled from North Carolina to Kansas. During the long commute, we ran out of gas at one point and were, quite literally, stuck on the side of the interstate, about five miles from the nearest gas station, with a three-year-old in the car. It was not safe for us to walk, so we immediately used the technology we had available and called a local service station. After about forty-five minutes of waiting and an extra sixty dollars for the delivery of some gas (which my father referred to as a "duh fee"), we were on our way to the next exit for a fill-up. The best part was that a three-year-old will never keep your secrets, so within five minutes of arriving at our family's place in Kansas, my daughter was telling them all about our low-fuel misadventure. My dad and I could only laugh and smile as she innocently shared her favorite part, the duh fee. For her, running out of gas was an exciting part of the trip, and it built a memory for her of a person she loved. Because of this guiding principle, we immediately accepted the situation and moved on to having fun while we waited. We were able to enjoy our forty-five minutes of waiting for gas with laughter rather than ill words and worry. We actually had a little fun and laughed as we called my mom to tell her it was her fault we ran out of gas in Kentucky the day after we left her in North Carolina; she was, after all, the one who was known for reminding Dad when the gas gauge was half-full. I, on the other hand, just rode, talked, laughed, sang, and listened and believed he was capable of guarding the gauge, which he obviously wasn't without Mom's input. What duh fees have you had to pay? Speeding ticket? Fender-benders? Extra charges for an overdue bill? Interest charges? Again, these are things you cannot change after the fact, so you must accept them and do whatever it takes to move on.

My twins were born prematurely and required longer hospital stays in a Neonatal Intensive Care Unit (NICU) that was an hour away from our house. My oldest son was five years old at the time and went to visit them in the hospital; as a result, he ended up at one himself, where he stayed a week to be treated for bacterial pneumonia. Accepting the things I could not change during those rough times meant making some adjustments for our family. Since my husband and I required sleep and needed to stay strong and healthy for our four children, three of whom were in the hospital, we huddled and came up with a new plan. My oldest, being only five, would not let us leave him in the room alone and did not even want us to close the bathroom door if we had to go. He was sick and in a scary, unfamiliar environment, surrounded by scrub-wearing strangers, and he was way out of his comfort zone. My parents and our friends, Beth, Jimmy, and Laura, went to visit the twins each day and hold them so my husband could stay the night at the hospital with my son and I could stay during the daytime. I returned home to sleep at night, and he slept there during the day. We called the hospital to be updated about the twins by the nurses and doctors but could not physically be there with them. No, it was not an ideal situation, but we were both smart enough not to deplete ourselves.

My oldest daughter was put in the care of friends and family who arranged her care without having to consent with us. We trusted them to handle the decisions of who would pick her up and when and where she would go. Since we'd already made the decision to leave her in the care of people we trusted, we did not need to micromanage their decisions; we knew if Karlee or they needed us, they would call. We knew there was a group of people in place who were working it all out for my daughter, and she had a party the whole time. Only eighteen months old, she was clueless about all that was going on with her brothers and sister, and she was happy because she was getting lots of attention from several people whom she knew and loved.

This guiding principle can also help with the everyday, mundane issues as well. For example, a friend was completely irritated by her husband's noncompliance when it came to picking up after himself. She came to the conclusion one day that she had a choice: She could allow his dirty socks to ruin her day or not. Once she chose to accept the situation and began picking up the socks in a happy mood, she found that he became more helpful. He actually began taking care of things before she could. Due to those improvements, her life became more enjoyable because she learned to accept him because she cannot change him. Complaining, whining, yelling, and screaming usually does not bring about any permanent change.

We face similar issues in my house, and I'm sure other married couples do as well. I have had to accept that my husband truly does not notice the same messes I do, but by the same token, I do not notice when one of the many trees in our yard needs to be trimmed or cut down. If I say, "I'm so tired. I'm going to bed," chances are that on the way, I'll finish the dishes, start the dishwasher, put away some toys, get the backpacks ready, and carry dirty clothes to the laundry room long before I eventually walk into my bedroom for the night. My husband, on the other hand, walks right in there, bypassing all of those household chores without even thinking to touch any of them. Thankfully, I've learned that I can't change him, and when I finally accepted that, he also accepted that I like certain things done around the house, and he now works to make sure that at least those things are done.

With four kids, I have had to accept that if I want to do something besides clean, I have to let the cleaning go. I do not apologize for the mess; if I was truly sorry, the mess would be gone, but at my house currently, the mess only leaves right after we pick it up. Within an hour or a day or two, it is back. I accept that one day, I will have four kids capable of doing more cleaning, but until then, I have a choice: I can let the mess make me miserable, or I can enjoy life regardless of the mess. Of course I am human, so the mess does overwhelm me at times, just not nearly as often as it once would have.

Like many, we have created credit card debt in the past, only for it to get out of control. In those instances, I had to accept that the financial mess did not happen overnight, and it would not be solved overnight. I had to accept that I made poor choices and make changes that will prevent the same in the future.

It is amazing to watch the life of some who are diagnosed with a disease or live life with a handicap. They understand that they must accept what they cannot change.

Their physical condition may force them to live differently or even make sacrifices, but they choose to live in the moment rather than to dwell on what they cannot change or to dwell in the past or what has already occurred.

The Courage to Change the Things You Can

Most people do not like change, even though it is an undeniable, essential part of life. It occurs over and over in many different ways. Within the first twenty-one years of life, we go through many changes, and these changes affect our parents' lives as well:

- Crawling
- Walking
- Potty-Training
- School
- Driving
- Graduation
- College

- Jobs

- Moving Out

An incredible friend taught me that life can still be lived, regardless of circumstances. Despite her devastating cancer diagnosis, she continued to teach, running to radiation treatments while her students went to music. Her cancer went into a brief remission, but when it came back, she did not want a blanket statement to be made. She just wanted to continue living her life. She was tired of always being asked how she was doing; she wanted people to converse with her and her family about something other than her cancer. She also was tiring of the telephone game, information being misinterpreted by people and fed back to her friends or family, only to alarm them. She accepted her diagnosis and decided that the one thing she could change was what information was given out about her and her condition. She could not protect her family or herself from the cancer in her body and its eventual effect, but she could protect them from having to hear disconcerting news; she did this by being selective about the information that was given to others. She informed her close circle that we were never to lie but that she did not want us to share more than necessary to answer the question. She provided us with an excellent example; she went to appointments by herself and only told us what she felt comfortable sharing. She knew what she was facing, and she began to live with it. She courageously changed what she could, what she shared with others, and she had an outstanding way with words.

Something I had to eventually accept in my life was the death of my father. He was my best friend, my biggest cheerleader, my teacher, and my guide, especially when I wandered off the right path. There was nothing I could do to bring him back, to change the fact that he is no longer here on Earth with me. I could not change that my children were so young when he died and that my two youngest, only two, would have very little, if any, personal memories of him. I could not change that my seven-year-old son, the oldest, was devastated by the loss. He loved his grandpa's black truck and shared his interest in vintage cars. I could not change that his grandpa is gone, but I could help him cope with the loss, and I continue to keep his memories strong by talking about their special moments.

As a direct result, I also had to accept that my mom is now a widow. Those first days with family in town, she always had someone in the house with her, but when everyone left, it broke my heart to be the last one to walk out the door. I offered to stay, of course, but she assured me she would be okay. I had to accept that she would be alone, in an empty house, because I couldn't change it, but I knew this same principle guided her. I knew my mother would accept the loss of her husband in time and, despite the difficulty, that she would embrace the next step and find the courage to change the things she could.

Change is not easy, and it does require great courage. Oftentimes, it brings with it fear, anxiety, stress (both good and bad), uncertainty, and many feelings of inadequacy or not being good enough. If we bow down to our feelings, change will never happen, and we will continue along in the same manner in which we are currently living.

I had reached a point in life when I was no longer happy. I was married, with one child, working a full-time job for which I'd been college educated, yet I was depressed and wanted to shed myself of my husband. Something had to change, and I knew I could no longer live the way I was living. I was completely empty on the inside, even if everything looked wonderful on the outside. I was extremely scared to make changes, but the fear of my life staying the same scared me more; therefore, I had to find the courage to change the things I could, because I knew the only way my situation would improve would be if I took the initiative and brought about the change myself. My defining moment was when I said to myself, "There is a God in heaven, and He doesn't want me to be miserable, so what's the problem?" I didn't know exactly what to do, so I started by selecting a book and reading someone else's story; I knew I could learn from the author, who had experienced more success and had more knowledge and more wisdom than me.

I continued making changes in my life and found that I was adding all kinds of tools to my tool belt in the process. Most importantly, I discovered that *I* was the problem, not my husband, Bobby, as I'd originally thought. I gained lots of knowledge through reading and my own experiences, and before I knew it, I was creating the life I wanted, one I can now say that I love. But the first and hardest step was to find the courage to change the things I could. What do you need to change? What in your life is not how you like it? What is causing you problems?

One of the things I needed to change was to make a way for me to stay home to raise my child. At the time, I was working all day, giving everything I had to my job, with nothing left to give to my family. I had always planned to be a stay-at-home mom, but two years into my motherhood, I had not fulfilled that dream. So, despite the fact that on paper, we couldn't afford for me not to work, I found the courage to change. Since then, I've found jobs that allow me to work from home on a flexible schedule, and over seven years later, I continue to work from home. It hasn't been easy. Being self-employed can be terrifying, and we had to adjust our spending and our priorities to make it work, but the courage to make that change has allowed me to live the life of my dreams and not someone else's. It has also allowed my husband and me to grow together as a team, rather than functioning as opponents or individuals.

The Wisdom to Know the Difference

We all like to believe we are in control and that we can make things happen. Truthfully, we can only change the things we see in the mirror. If you are like me, along life's journey, you will stubbornly try to change things that you cannot. You will accept things, but only those you can change, and when you try to change the things you cannot, they will come back to bite you. It takes courage to change the things you can, but it also takes wisdom to realize the things you can't.

I once thought I could change someone else's situation. I hopped into their hula hoop and tried to tell them, in a nice way, what they needed to do. That person has not spoken to me in over ten years, and I don't blame them. I hope one day they will find the ability to forgive me for my mistake, but I have apologized and accepted my responsibility in the situation. I must also accept the consequences, because I cannot change their decision to forgive or not. I did not have the necessary wisdom, and I thought I could change something that I actually needed to accept. It was an excellent lesson on my life journey, but it cost me a good friend.

I was able to see what I thought my friend was doing wrong, but meanwhile, I was completely unaware of how depressed and unhappy I was in my own personal life. Hurting people hurt others; in this example, I was a hurting person who brought hurt to someone else because I lacked wisdom to know the difference, but it was also because I was ignoring what was going on in my own hula hoop and choosing to get in theirs instead.

Often I see, hear, and work with people who spend their time trying to change things they cannot change. They try to change their spouse, children (of course there is a difference in raising and disciplining a child and trying to change them), friends, co-workers, bosses, etc. Like I was in the above situation, they are convinced that their way is the right way and that the other needs to change. Trying to change things that actually need to be accepted reveals a lack of wisdom.

I also see the opposite, people accepting things they actually have the ability to change. Some things you have the ability to change in your life include:

- Your attitude

- Your financial situation

- Drama in your life

- Your job

- Your relationships

- Too much on your calendar

- How you deal with situations

- Allowing others to treat you poorly

A friend of mine once shared that she had a friend who called her at ten p.m. She said, "I go to bed at nine, and if someone is calling at ten, my first instinct is that it's an emergency." When the person called, she didn't answer the phone and let the answering machine get it, even though she was awake. She listened to make sure it wasn't an emergency, and it wasn't. The next day the person said, "I tried to call you last night," but my friend responded, "I know. I was in bed."

The truth is, we teach people how to treat us. Her simple approach taught this person that if she wanted to talk to her, she needed to call earlier. Had she chosen to answer the phone when her friend called, the friend would have continued calling at that time.

We have the ability to change how people treat us by simply changing our response to their behavior. You hold the key to the solutions of your problems in your response. Sometimes it is necessary to exert self-control by saying nothing, walking away, standing up, being honest, saying no, or forgiving someone or something. As you may already know, it is not good to start a conversation with, "Don't be mad, but…" or "I probably shouldn't say this…"

or "So-and-so told me that…" None of these are likely to bring about good responses.

I have the greatest marriage now because Bobby and I have both changed how we respond to each other. We have learned how one another prefers to be treated, and we do our best to honor these differences. Of course there are occasions when the stresses of life throw us off our game. We may be tired, sick, or overwhelmed, or there could be any number of reasons we respond to each other in an inappropriate way, resulting in a squabble. But this, too, is quickly overcome because we recognize what has occurred, and we don't continue to pour fuel on the fire. I recall times when I purposefully poured gas on the fire just to get another jab in at my husband, but now we have taken time to understand each other; in turn, the majority of time, we communicate in very healthy ways. We are aware of one another's needs, and we strive to ensure that those needs are being met. We have gained the wisdom to know that we can change our relationship, and we have also gained the wisdom to know which parts we can change and which we must accept. The truth is, I no longer try to change my husband because I have the wisdom to know I can't. I must accept him for who he is.

I do have the power to change how his actions make me feel, because I am in control of my feelings, and I am also aware of how he operates. While I may feel he meant something a certain way, that may not have been his intention. Our feelings are real, but they are not necessarily reality.

> ## Your feelings are REAL
> ## BUT
> ## not necessarily REALITY.

My husband could tell you exactly how many times he's gone hunting in the last week, month, and year, but there were times when I would argue with him, claiming that he was always hunting, because that was how I felt. I have adopted a new saying, because my feelings have caused me a lot of unnecessary pain and suffering over the years. I was, most definitely, the type who wore her feelings on her sleeve, where they were very vulnerable and out in the open. I began to say, "I am not saying it is reality, but this is how I feel." This allowed for much healthier conversation between us, because my husband never intended to hurt my feelings; it happened without him even being aware. This statement did not put him on the defensive, so we didn't experience fights and arguments, which wouldn't have solved anything. Instead, he now understood what I was feeling, and he was able and willing to help me through irrational feelings that were hindering my life and happiness and his. He also learned that there were things he could tweak (change) to prevent these irrational feelings from spiking. He loved me enough to choose to understand me, and that meant understanding *all* of me.

My old way of handling things was to blame him and his actions for causing me pain, when the fact was that I was actually causing my own pain. My perceptions were not necessarily reality. Even though they seemed real to me, they were incorrect feelings. This happens far too often in relationships, and it breaks my heart when marriages end in divorce because:

- The couple simply does not communicate or does so in an unhealthy, damaging manner.
- Each tries to change things they can't.
- They claim life is wonderful and that they are okay when they are not
- The individuals blame each other unjustifiably.
- They act and speak selfishly
- One or both parties fail to put forth any effort into the relationship and making it work.

Often ask yourself, "Are these just feelings, or is this reality?" I have found that many people confuse the two, summoning unnecessary troubles to their lives. A very depressed man believed his wife was having an affair because she had been out two nights in a row, claiming she was with friends. He asked me, "What would you think?" Since I had actually been with his wife on one of the nights, I knew she was telling him the truth. My first instinct was to laugh at him and tell him he was being ridiculous and overreacting, but then I saw the look in his eyes. His broken spirit and tear-filled eyes let me know quickly that he was 100 percent serious and believed it to be true. I changed my response and repeated to him what I had learned to say to my husband: "Those are your feelings, and they are real, but it is not necessarily reality."

Bobby and I can speak from experience, and we would both tell you that once you choose to understand one another, it is much easier to accept one another's quirks and differences. My weaknesses no longer make him angry; rather, they make him grin and giggle because he realizes how irrational they are. Still, because he knows they are very real to me, he wants to help me through them rather than letting them stop me. We have helped one another to grow into a greater, happier, healthier life. We now truly accept one another for better and for worse.

I encourage you to write out the Serenity Prayer and post it on your bathroom mirror, in your car, on your desk, on the fridge, and anywhere else that you will see it often. In these amazing, insightful words, there is so much untapped power for an amazing life. Even if you are not a believer or a praying person, you can still learn to accept the things you cannot change, find the courage to change the things you can, and discern the wisdom to know the difference—some of the greatest practical advice ever given.

CHAPTER 2

T.I.M.E: Things I Must Experience

"Love and time are the only two things in this world that cannot be bought, only spent."

~ Gary Jennings

People often want to know how I keep a good, positive outlook, especially in my darkest times. The answer is quite simple: I accept that what I am going through is something I must experience in order to prepare me for something else or something more in the future.

I want to be open to all the lessons presented to me as I do not want to have to go through something again because I missed out on a lesson. I look at all obstacles as opportunities to learn. Perhaps it is to teach me to be patient or to avoid letting mishaps or mistakes consume my energy. If it seems as if I am circling the same mountain and not climbing, I ask Kelly and Bobby, my innermost circle, "Am I missing something?" Sometimes it is just things I must experience (T.I.M.E.). Sometimes I need to make a tweak, a simple shift in thoughts, actions, responses, or words.

When my washing machine began to leak for the fourth time in less than two years, I sent my husband a rather humorous text: "Great news. Either the washing machine is leaking, or someone peed on the floor." I knew I didn't have to let the leaky machine ruin my day, my week, or my month. It did not need to be the new topic of my conversations when I spoke to someone. I couldn't change it, so I had to accept it and decide what to do next.

Looking back, my reaction of literally jumping from the bed and releasing an excited cheer was probably not the best choice when I learned that Bobby had been terminated from his job, but at the time, I did not realize the extent of his initial hurt. In many people's minds there was no acceptable reason for the termination, since there was no previous disciplinary action, but it did allow for opportunity for something else. He had devoted nearly fifteen and a half years to the agency, and his team was on his mind twenty-four/seven, able to call him anytime, day or night. He had struggled to accept his termination, and I should have bit my tongue a little bit to contain my excitement, but it didn't take me too long to realize it, so I quickly reined myself in. Things would be different for him and for us, but I knew different didn't have to mean bad. I knew we were going to gain more than we were losing. Had it happened several years earlier, I would not have handled the situation the same, but because of the T.I.M.E. I'd gone through before, I was prepared with a positive attitude. After the initial shock wore off, Bobby was positive about it as well. We accepted the things we could not change and dug deeper for the courage to change the things we could.

My dad experienced some of the same feelings. He devoted forty years of his life to General Motors to keep the shop going and the machines running, often pulling over-, double-, or even triple-time. He was compensated well for his hours of labor, but he shed tears when they tore down the plant he had dedicated his life to. Thankfully, he was already in retirement, but the facility he'd faithfully devoted all those years to was suddenly flattened into a parking lot. Both men, my father and my husband, had poured hours of work and thought into their places of work, but in the end, they realized that what had been so important to them was not as important to someone else.

When my dad became sick, I could have chosen to point an accusatory finger in a variety of directions, since a series of medical decisions had only served to worsen the severity of his condition. However, because my thoughts were not clouded with worry, anger, or frustration, I could see that the doctors working on my dad's case had the utmost concern in their eyes. They didn't need me to point out what was already known, and I felt they were making the best decisions they could at the time, with the best of intentions. They had no way of predicting what would happen next.

Dad's personal physician visited the hospital before his regular office hours and on his lunch break as well, and during a few of those visits, I saw tears filling his eyes. I went to see that doctor just after my dad died. He came into the room and immediately gave me all the answers he thought I was there to hear. I started to interrupt him, but realized I needed to be quiet and let him speak. When he finished, I reached over, placed my hand on his arm, and said, "My dad died because it was his time to die. I only came today to tell you not to question yourself in the future. You are a great doctor." The look on his face was almost one of relief. I can only imagine the amount of hours he lost sleep, thinking about my dad and all the what-ifs connected with his case. What the good doctor didn't know was that Dad and I had had many conversations about faith, God, and the end of one's days on Earth, and we both believed that his time would come in His time, regardless of the surrounding circumstances.

I will always miss my father and wish he was back in my life, but I am also thankful that he did not have to battle through the tough physical road that was ahead of him. He had already battled alcoholism each and every day for twenty-five years. He had already endured and fought against the daily effects of his diabetes, lupus, and other medical conditions. He had already given so unselfishly, not only to his immediate family, but also to anyone who was placed in his path. He had already understood and put T.I.M.E. into practice, and he took those experiences and the lessons learned and passed them on to anyone who would listen. He had suffered through the rejection of sharing his heart with someone who was not ready and having to watch them continue to suffer. My dad was survived by three older brothers and his mother, and while he did not go in the natural order we think family members should go, I am thankful that he went out at the top of his game.

I was once told that I tend to look through rose-colored glasses. The funny thing to me is that the person who said it clearly did not intend it as a compliment; nevertheless, I was quite proud they thought that of me. In response, I explained that the Bible tells us that God is a God of abundance. This does necessarily have anything to do with money, though He does own the whole world and every penny in it. What it does mean is that He can grant us an abundance of peace, grace, mercy, love, and hope. I also explained that He promises never to give me more than I can carry. This is exactly why I can laugh at my biggest obstacles and say, "Oh my! I can't believe how strong He thinks I am!" There will always be storms, but I just allow

Him to carry me through as He tells me He will. I also explained that what is meant for evil will be used for good for those who love the Lord.

Feelings, circumstances, obstacles, and being human can get in the way of the execution of this abundance in our lives. People may believe something in the morning but completely let go of those reins by afternoon. You may get knocked down, but if you believe strongly in your guiding principles, T.I.M.E will allow you to keep hold of the reins as you are walking through the lesson. Then you can get back up, look back, and say, "That was an incredible ride, and I'm thankful for it, but I don't want to take it again!" You will take with you the lessons the experience gives you, and the rest will settle as dust on the trail.

When you accept the things you cannot change, it allows you to enjoy your trials, your time in the valley, your hurdles, and your obstacles. Your biggest obstacles will become comical when you begin to understand that it is just part of the process, the things you must experience. Many of the things I do today are a direct result of T.I.M.E.

I just ask that you begin to make the next step to accepting the events in your life as things you must experience. You will not understand it now, but later you will be able to look back and see that because you learned from it, you can now face a bigger mountain.

Stop giving your T.I.M.E. away, and really embrace them for the lessons being offered. Obstacles will never stop, but how you approach and respond to the obstacle can change if you are willing to grow into it. If I tried to run a hurdle course on foot, I'd probably fall flat on my face, but I can gladly say that for facing life's hurdles, I have developed a pretty amazing rhythm, and you can too! Keep an eye on how you react to things. I used to react with sleep to avoid reality, and if I allowed it, I would still turn to that as a coping mechanism. However, now that I recognize it, I can change it. I know I must dig in, find the courage to face the situation, and accept it as T.I.M.E.

Investing Your Time to Enhance Your T.I.M.E.

People have different talents and varying levels of skill; however, we all get the same number of hours in a day. What you do with those twenty-four hours is up to you. You cannot save, trade, or buy more time. Once a minute is gone, it is gone forever. There is an end, and everyone will eventually run out of precious time. The goal should be that we accomplish things and enjoy life, rather than reaching the end and realizing we missed out on many opportunities. I've wasted many of my precious minutes being upset, feeling hurt, dwelling in fear, and trying to predict the future. When I learned about what time really is, I became much more diligent about protecting mine.

It should be obvious that time is something we should be very careful about, but it is something many people don't even think about. Typically, the only time when time comes up in conversation is when someone is complaining that they don't have enough of it, yet very little effort is exerted by most people to figure out how to effectively use their time. Have you looked at your weekly plan to figure out where your time is going? Do you even have a weekly plan? After I looked at my life on a plan sheet, it was easy to begin capitalizing on lost time, wasted time, and invested time. Once you have a plan in place, know that at certain stages in your life, you may need to revisit that plan and make changes; remember that you need to accept what you cannot change and have the courage to make the positive changes you can.

For example, during my high school years, I had more time for sports practice and hanging out with my friends. In my college years, I had more time for socializing, studying, and hanging out and playing games. In my early career years as a single young adult, I only had to be concerned with my needs as far as income, bills, and entertainment. Then came marriage.

For several years, my husband and I often went out to dinner with friends. I often left work and went shopping with a friend. When I had a child, I had to cut into some of that time; I now had to honor my son's naptime and bedtime, which left me alone in a quiet house. I had to adjust. I was no longer satisfied with giving the best of me to my job, so I had to find the courage to change and work from home, adjusting our bills and lifestyle to accommodate my revised desires. I was able to take my son to the library and play groups. When my oldest daughter was born, I continued some of those activities, but I had to adjust to her routine as well. Then, a short time later, I gave birth to two more children, and my public outings consisted of doctor's appointments and church. I felt as if I was losing touch, and I had a need for social interaction that required revisiting my weekly plan to find space to fill that need. I don't always make the right decisions in life, and I knew I hadn't, because I slowly began to lose my grip on sanity. At that point, I realized I had to revamp the schedule again. I almost fall over when I discovered that in less than a year's time, I could gain about thirty-five hours a week of uninterrupted time, though it would require making sure my time was invested wisely and not simply wasted.

Your life is no different. Perhaps you have no children, only one child, or thirteen children. Maybe you work fifty hours a week outside of the home. Somewhere, you might be squeezing in a thirty-minute slot for a workout or your commute to work. What is important to you in your life may very well differ from what's important to me in mine. All that matters is that you have a plan that works for you, one that will fit your needs and accommodate your lifestyle, whatever that includes.

First, let's look at how much time we actually have: 1 day, 24 hours, results in 1,440 minutes. If you give 8 hours (480 minutes) a day to work and 8 to sleep, you still have 8 hours left each day. That's enough for a second forty-hour/week job. While most people don't want to moonlight as a way to fill in their time, you could use those eight hours every day enjoying any of the following:

- Physical activity
- Outings with friends
- That second job if you do need extra income
- Quality time with family, kids, and those you love
- Hobbies and activities
- Cleaning and catching up on household projects

There are also plenty of time-stealers. These are either a complete waste of your time, and even good things can be time-stealers if you are not careful. If mismanaged, even seemingly effective or positive things can spin out of control and waste your time. These can include everything from technology to emotions:

- Cell phone

- Videogames

- Social media

- Reading

- Television

- Worry

- Anger

I often teach others how to develop a plan. It is easy to serve as a facilitator and trainer and pass on this knowledge, but I cannot tell another individual what they need to do. I am often able to talk someone through it, but the ultimate decision in creating and executing the plan lies with you. The important thing is getting your plan working for you and not against you.

Make sure you are spending your time where it counts. Sometimes I have to crack the whip on myself because my need for social interaction gets out of whack, and I find myself wasting time on social media. Sometimes, when I'm not reading in a disciplined way, I go on an overdrive reading spree, causing me to neglect all other things. I sometimes rely on these time-stealers as distractions, to help me avoid doing or facing something that is difficult or scary for me. I am a procrastinator, so solid deadlines seem to work well for me. I am also easily distracted and can easily go off on rabbit trails, wasting rather than investing my time. I have had to learn to face my emotions and do it anyway. In turn, I have learned that I can do more. I am good enough just the way I am, as long as I continue to self-manage, self-discipline, and grow. The obstacle of time will always be there and needs to be checked to ensure that you haven't slipped into wasting rather than investing.

What have you learned from your hurdles? I have learned that I am good enough being me, but another lesson I've had to learn is that I cannot be affected by other people's choices. I also know that I must be accountable to the details. I am really great when it comes to big ideas, but the actual execution and attention to detail has always been difficult for me. Goal-setting and accountability partners have helped to keep me on track. Rather than using my weaknesses as a crutch, I have instead found ways through the things I have experienced, to become a stronger person. I also had to learn that happiness comes from within me; previously, I looked for it through external stimuli, but I seldom ever found it. Now, I could be happy on a deserted island if I chose to be. All of these lessons came from T.I.M.E., and the hurdles are necessary for the experience you will need in the future.

My grandma once asked my dad if all his troubles had to happen for him to become who he was. My dad was certain that all of it, every step of the way, was necessary. Without the tough lessons, he never would have been able to help others through their tough times. He assisted many people outside of AA, but he also touched countless lives, those negatively affected by the same disease he'd suffered with, because he'd walked in their shoes. He could relate to their situation, and he was more than willing to share his experiences to help them gain more understanding as to how they might solve their own problems. My dad gleaned much from his T.I.M.E., and he passed those lessons on. Today, you and I can do the same.

CHAPTER 3

Be Thankful for What You Don't Have

"Some people are always grumbling because roses have thorns. I am thankful that thorns have roses."

~ Alphonse Karr

Sitting at Gina's, in my hometown of Flushing, Michigan my dad and I made plans to shop for a car. I was nearing the completion of my college education and would soon be starting my career. We couldn't wait for me to graduate, because my previous clunker had already clunked out. As I sat there, dreaming of the perfect car, my dad said, "Be thankful for what you don't have." I looked at him as if he was trying to burst my bubble, so he elaborated, "Every car comes with a price tag. In the past, you haven't had a car payment to make, because it was under $1,000 and we could pay for it out of pocket. Now, you'll have a monthly payment." He saw my excitement and envy when I looked at some of my friends' cars, but he also understood much more than I did at the ripe old age of twenty-one.

I am often reminded of that moment when I try to achieve something before it is time and end up drowning in debt. Large bills can make life miserable and steal our joy. Being overburdened with payments can make us feel defeated, as if we'll forever be attached to a ball and chain.

I am also reminded of this story when someone has something I don't, which could be good or bad. I am thankful I don't have cancer, a shopping addiction, or a beach house, since I couldn't possibly handle the upkeep of such a place with all that I already have on my plate. I am also thankful I am not a compulsive liar, an alcoholic, or drug addict. I am even thankful I don't have a horse; as much as much as I would love to take up an equestrian hobby, I recognize that I don't have the time in my life right now to accommodate this desire, and it would be more of a burden than an enjoyment. I would love a pool and plan to one day have one installed, but now is simply not the right time. While you're thinking of what you do want out of life, be sure to remember to be thankful for the things you don't have because they would not be good for you, at least not now.

I have found that being thankful for what I don't have prevents me from judging others and keeps me humble. Instead of insulting a drug addict, for instance, I can be thankful I have not had to walk in their shoes. Instead of gossiping about those who are trying to harm me, I can be thankful that my life is not consumed with tearing someone else down. Their actions may still be frustrating, but I am able to be thankful that I am not that way because I've learned that their chosen way of life brings only pain and suffering. I don't have to be angry at anyone for their actions. I actually feel sorry for them because I am grateful that I don't have to live or feel that way. I have learned that what people do to tear another down is nothing compared to what it is doing to them in the process.

When others are beaten down about what they don't have, I am actually upbeat. I can be thankful for what I don't have because I recognize why I don't have it. I have even been thankful for being without an abundance of money because I knew I would not be skilled or wise enough to handle it. The abundance would have only brought more trouble into my life than I was ready for.

I am thankful that when I lay my head down at night, I can drift off to sleep without a bunch of junk turning and churning in my head. I am thankful that when I wake up, I can confidently go about life the best way I know how. If someone doesn't agree with it, that's okay, because I'm meant to walk in my path, not theirs.

Today's troubled economy means too many people having too much credit and nothing in the bank. Too many are quicker to fill out a credit card application instead of an application for a savings account. In a society of buy-now-pay-later thinking and instant gratification, we do not teach our children how to be disciplined and save. Therefore, when jobs started going away, no one was prepared to cover three months' worth of bills. The rainy days have come, but no one has anything saved back for it.

Consider a very simple person who pays only with cash, bought their car outright, and owns no credit cards. If such a person loses their job, at the very most, they will need to cover the mortgage, food, utilities. The truth is, if we were all this smart and disciplined, an economic crisis wouldn't be nearly as daunting; if the house and car were paid for, we would only have to provide food, warmth, and light, two of which could be done by burning a fire. The basics, to the average American today, are far excessive of what was viewed as basics in years gone by. For instance, cell phones are no longer considered a luxury but are viewed as a necessity. Home Internet access is also considered a necessity, even though the Web can be accessed in public libraries and other places at no cost. Please don't misunderstand: There is nothing wrong with having things, but with that comes the necessity to be prepared to meet your needs in case of an emergency such as a job loss, illness, or the death of a provider. We cannot stand there scratching our heads, wondering what to do, and shaking our fist at our employer when the ultimate problem is that our bills exceed our savings and income and what we were barely paying before we are not able to pay at all.

When the news came that we no longer had an income, we were able to sustain ourselves rather easily for four months. The fifth and six month were a bit more difficult, and that was complicated by the fact that we knew the new income was out there but was just not necessarily in our hands. We should have endured longer, but we made a couple of choices that didn't turn out to be the best we could have made.

No matter what, be thankful for what you don't have. Don't judge a pregnant teenager; instead, be thankful that you are not dealing with that type of difficult situation in your home. Don't judge the thief; just be thankful you choose not to steal.

Living paycheck to paycheck can be miserable. I have done it all too often and would not wish it on anyone. Those who have some savings, whether in a bank or in a shoebox under the bed, are at least somewhat prepared for emergencies and unexpected necessaries, such as the car breaking down, a trip that must be taken, or a new pair of glasses when the others get smashed on the playground. Being prepared for mishaps, which will happen as long as you are breathing, is a way to keep peace in your life.

My Uncle George shared something about stuff with my grandma, and she passed this important message on to me during one of our conversations: "When it comes to stuff, we store 80 percent and use 20." If you don't believe this is true, consider the size of closets and storage areas in houses today vs. fifty years ago. Think about all the storage units and hoarding shows you might see on TV. We are a very stuff-oriented society. I am not a shopper, but through gifts and hand-me-downs from others, my son now has over sixty short-sleeved shirts in his closet. I could understand this if I was a compulsive shopper, but I didn't purchase one shirt for the start of his school year. He doesn't care much about fashion, and even with all those selections, he still wears the same few shirts week in and week out. If he wore a different shirt every day, his wardrobe would carry him through two months.

I do go through our stockpile of stuff often and donate several times a year, yet plenty of stuff still lingers in my home. So many people are overrun with clutter, to the point of having to buy extra buildings or rent storage space just to house it. Not only does stuff clutter our world, but it also clutters the mind. Those around me know I am always battling the mounds of stuff that invades my house; I do not want to waste my time having to dig through it to find what I really want or need. Do yourself a favor: Purge the stuff! Then, when you're finished, feel free to come and lend me a hand with my pile, because as the mother of four, I seem to be drowning in a never-ending pile of stuff! Please don't think I am ungrateful, as I am very thankful for all we have been blessed with, but the overabundance of useless or unnecessary things around me causes stress in my life. As a lover of serenity, I work hard to keep all the extras out, and I try to remain ever thankful for all that I do not have!

> # STUFF=
> ## 80% we store - 20% we use

CHAPTER 4

Doing Their Best

"We cannot hope to scale great moral heights by ignoring petty obligations."

~ Agnes Repplier

One way to maintain peace in your life is to try to understand that most people are doing the best they can. I do not have to get mad when someone does something I don't agree with. Instead, I simply remind myself that they are simply doing the best they can in their situation, with the resources they have been given. During my own life, I have unintentionally hurt people by making unwise choices, wasting time, wasting money, yelling too loud, or disciplining ineffectively. It doesn't take me long to find something I could have changed about my day, a different choice I could have made, a different way I could have handled a situation. The bottom line, though, is that I've always tried to do the best I can.

It is important to realize, though, that being good enough or doing your best is not a license to say, "This is just the way I am, so deal with it." No, doing the best you can simply means being the best you can be today, yet always striving, through self-discipline and a willingness to do so, to grow into something better. Also, once you become aware of a behavior that needs to be adjusted, it is your responsibility to change, not to rely on the excuse, "This is just the way I am."

Getting up in the morning is a challenge for me. If my children started school at 8:30 instead of 7:50 a.m., it would be easier for me to get them to school on time, but that is no excuse for me to be late. I must do my best to get them there on time, even if an early bird is not who I am.

While change and improvements are important, we must also learn to accept ourselves the way we are at a fundamental level. For many years, I was disappointed because I'd always enjoyed being a cheerleader, and I was sure there would be no place for that in my adult life. I have since learned that being a good cheerleader is perfect for what I am passionate about in my life. The paths I now take in life revolve around opportunities to capitalize on my strengths but also build on my weaknesses. I have found ways to provide an income through cheerleading and loving people, two things I am good at and enjoy.

It took many years and many tears, but I am now satisfied with who I am, and I have accepted that being me is good enough. Be confident in who you are and love yourself so you can properly love others. If you are unhappy with yourself, you will be unhappy with others. When you fully accept yourself for the good, the bad, and the ugly, you will more easily be able to accept these qualities and flaws in others.

I have learned to give this same respect to others. I am no better and no worse than anyone, for I've possibly done the same things in the past or very well may in the future. I have learned not to say, "I will never..." because I don't know the future and what will be presented to me. Instead, I choose to hold close to one of my dad's greatest gifts, allowing each person to be the best they can be in the moment. My father taught that the man at the homeless shelter and the Pope are both doing the best they can. Dad knew this, because he had walked in the same shoes as people who traverse a very rough road. What shoes have you walked in that could help another? What knowledge can you share from your T.I.M.E. to help others do their best?

I no longer have to get upset with whiners, complainers, moaners, and groaners. I was once that way, so I just remind myself that they are doing the best they can, and then I choose how to respond. Sometimes I pull back some of my contact with them or to give them time to vent so they can clear their heads and get back up and ride again.

At times, a person just needs to talk, or women may say they need a good cry. When someone is able to expel all their junk, they feel better, lighter, and ready to go again. Deflection and pushing through fears can cause us to set many feelings aside; over time, these can build up, and they must be released so they don't consume us from within. Of course my husband still does not understand how crying could ever be a good thing, but for me and others like me, it serves like the valve on a pressure cooker, releasing the internal steam that would otherwise hold me back from accomplishing all that has been set in front of me.

Every individual has a varying set of talents and skills. Over time, these skills are strengthened, and other skills may seem weak by comparison. If you don't exercise a skill, it will not become stronger. I see this often in how people handle their obstacles. Those who choose the easy route do not develop the muscles of patience, and a quick fix will not enhance one's strength or the ability to persevere.

It may not be the best you could do, but it is their journey, and it is different from yours. They may not have had the same experiences to learn from. An eighteen-year-old may believe he knows it all, but people in their thirties, forties, and fifties will criticize him for bad choices, even if they have had many more experiences to learn from. We cannot expect a four-year-old to do the math required of a first-grader, so why do we expect so much from people who are not yet capable of living up to those expectations? I must be careful, for I tend to be guilty of this, particularly when it comes to my kids' ability to clean or pick up after themselves. Sometimes, especially when I am tired, my expectations fall ridiculously above their skill levels. I have to tell myself time and time again that they are doing the best they can to make Mom happy.

Once someone becomes aware that there are other possibilities and tools out there to be used, that is when we go from doing our best to remaining ignorant. For example, I am known to be at peace when tornadoes are swirling around me, yet when I was facing one of my biggest life obstacles my mind was becoming clouded, and negative thoughts threatened to take over. Several times every minute, I had to employ deep-breathing techniques to exhale the junk out. My peace was being invaded, and while I could see what was happening, my fight against it seemed to be getting weaker. I recognized my personal signals and tried to grab all the resources I could from my tool belt, but they weren't nearly as effective as I hoped. Eventually, I looked at the three adults and four children in the room and said, "I'm going running." I hadn't been involved in physical exercise in twenty years, but I knew it might help, and I was willing to do anything to get my peace back. Anyone who has lived in peace will do anything to keep it from evaporating. Since I couldn't think of anything better to try, I laced up my tennis shoes and headed out the door.

I traveled about 2.4 miles that day. I was not in good enough shape to run the entire time, so I alternated between running and walking. My time, nothing to write the Olympic Committee about, was about forty-two minutes. If you are a runner, you might be laughing hysterically at that time, but it was the best I could do, and when I stopped using the curvy mountain road as an excuse, I got increasingly better within a week, cutting over ten minutes off that original time. For me, the first run was excellent, albeit more for accomplishment than any stellar athletic performance. I said to myself, "I'm going to start running here." By the time I was nearing the end of the run, I was telling myself, "You can do it! You can do it!" I had to push to get to that stopping mark, and I was out of breath when I got there, but I was proud that I'd made it. After a short recovery walk, I started again, with a new goal for myself. The sense of accomplishment I did not feel in my personal life was granted to me on that run, and I came back with a clear head because I'd chosen to dig deeper. With every pound of my foot on that pavement, another important lesson was pounded into my head and heart: Life is about recovery, about falling but getting back up.

My bounce-back (BB) rate has increased greatly over the last six years, so there is hope for my running time if I continue. I admit that I have fallen off the train a bit, but I may choose to get back on one day. There was a time in my life when I would sleep for hours when I thought someone was mad at me, just so I could avoid the feelings. Today, my BB rate for such a thing is 0 to 120 minutes. As I have said before, I have learned that my feelings are not necessarily reality. I no longer allow my feelings to steal the serenity of my life as they once did.

Many people want what others have but are unwilling to do what is necessary to get to that point. They are not willing to make the sacrifices that another has made. Many have said they envy my outlook on life, that they wish they could handle things with the ease that I do. However, when given the opportunity to participate in a training session, they have an excuse. I used to get mad and hurt when I took the time to prepare something and someone did not show up, but I've had to let those bitter feelings go. That person has their reasons for not being there, and they are doing the best they can. Besides, most of the time, there is someone else who is more than happy to learn, so I know my time was not wasted. It is their choice how long they will endure the struggle, not mine. The only burdens I can carry are mine, but I can love them in spite of their choices. They are the only one that can decide if the decision was right or wrong.

A wonderful friend of mine has dedicated many of her years to developing her skills in karate. Even after two children and nearing the forty-year-old mark, her body is quite remarkable, healthy, toned, and strong. People often say, "It must be nice," which is actually an underhanded jab, a stone thrown at her out of jealousy. It probably does feel great to be more fit than you were in high school, something I wouldn't know from experience, but she did not just magically wake up that way twenty years later. Wishful thinking has never gotten anyone anywhere. No, she was willing to sacrifice when others weren't, and she deserves what she has rightfully worked to create.

Even the drug addict is doing the best they can. There may come a time when they are strong enough to just say no to the addiction. You may not understand why they keep doing something that is breaking the family apart and destroying lives, but the bottom line is that they are still doing the best they can. Don't enable them by making their life easier. Hold them accountable. Don't let their choices dictate how you feel. Just love them anyway.

My husband has trained and adopted these ways of thinking, but there are still moments when we inadvertently revert back to our old ways of communicating. These usually occur when one of us is hungry, angry, lonely, tired, or confused. Sometimes I have to bite my tongue and get out of the way because he is confused or angry. Even if those feelings are not necessarily directed at me, if I try to engage him, I know I might end up being the target. Earlier in our marriage, this would have hurt my feelings, and I would have blamed myself and wasted precious time trying to figure out what I had done to deserve it. Now, I understand that he might just be going through something, and it has nothing to do with me personally. So, instead of wasting time worrying about it or stirring up the hornet's nest, I let him deal with it however he needs to.

We recently celebrated our anniversary. While I was getting ready, I was irritated at having to reorganize the kids' bedrooms due to all the clutter, which I despise. For a week, we couldn't find underwear, socks, or shorts, so I'd finally decided to take a moment to get things back in order. The entire time, I tried to tell myself not to be aggravated, but I knew my emotions were escalating. I did not want to be around people, because I knew that one wrong word might have me vomiting my anger all over them. My husband came in the room, and everything he said seemed to irritate me, even things that normally wouldn't have upset me; unbeknownst to him, I was not operating at my best, and I knew it. I was, however, operating the best I could in that moment, and I asked sternly, "Will you please stop and get out? I'm doing my best to keep from lashing out at you, but if you don't get away and hush, it's going to come out." I wanted to warn him that he was dancing atop a bubbling volcano that could blow any minute, and he understood and complied. Less than ten minutes later, I was ready to leave and was back to myself.

Sometimes when I get upset about something, I need to get away. This can be difficult for my husband. He used to block me so I couldn't get away and try to force me to talk about things, but that only enraged me and escalated my emotions until the whole situation morphed into a show that I wasn't proud of. He has learned that he has to go against what he wants in order to give me those moments I need so I can handle the situation rationally. This might involve just going to the bedroom and reading for three minutes; even that might allow me to get realigned. He doesn't like it because he feels uncomfortable for those minutes, but he knows that in order for things to be sensible, it is a requirement. Over time, he has learned to handle and appreciate this, and when I become irrational, he asks, "Honey, do you want to go read? I'll watch the kids." When he makes this comment, it is a sign to me that my stress level is noticeably out of whack, and I am not being my best me. We all do the best we can in the moment, and sometimes that means stepping away.

CHAPTER 5

Responsibility

"You are responsible for your life. You can't keep blaming somebody else for your dysfunction. Life is really about moving on."

~ Oprah Winfrey

When I began teaching elementary school in 1999, I asked my dad, "Where has responsibility gone?" The way I recall my parents responding to school issues was completely different than what I was experiencing as a teacher, on the other side of the fence. I was completely amazed to discover what parents openly discussed in front of their children about the school, other students, teachers, and principals. In fact, the hardest part about being a teacher was dealing with parents. Some seemed to view me as an enemy, even though my goal was simply to collaborate with them to raise their child into a responsible adult. Most of the parents I encountered were helpful and kind, but I was surprised by the some of the comments directed at me from parents, as well as the things my fellow teachers endured.

One incident I still recall revealed the lengths some parents will go to to protect their child from responsibility. At the completion of one of the school programs, students were to receive a certificate and t-shirt. One particular student struggled greatly in school, in both behavior and academics. I really liked the student but truly feared the wrath of his mother. The student was in jeopardy of not receiving his certificate due to his behavior not only in my class but also in a couple others as well. The principal, mother, father, student, and I met. While I sat quietly, they explained to the boy that he had less than a week left and one chance to make it to graduation. Four adults reiterated the consequences for any misbehavior. We operated off a card system for the week, starting with green, then moving to yellow, orange, red, and finally blue. If he lost all of his cards, he would not be able to participate. He was already on red, as two of his cards had been pulled by another teacher. The principal asked her to give back one of the cards, and while she didn't agree that she should, she honored the principal's request, and the student was back to orange, with two days to go.

On the final day, he was down to his blue card. The principal pulled him out of class to remind him that he had to make it through the day. A little while later, he had been given a Christmas trinket from a special teacher. He showed it to me, and I said, "That's great, but you need to put it in your book bag right now so it won't get you into trouble." Less than five minutes later, the toy went sailing across the classroom like a rocket. I had warned the child about the toy, and he was aware of the consequences of acting up in class, so I had to pull his last and final card and send him to the office, where he would be informed that he would not receive his certificate.

I was later informed that the mother and principal agreed that he would be paddled instead and that he would graduate from the program. This proved to the child that what all those adults had told him didn't matter, giving him no reason to listen to rules or warnings in the future. By our actions, we had shown him we were willing to change our minds.

I literally went home and cried. Was I the only one who really cared about the boy's future? Did they not see that the lack of accountability would continue, that the child would now feel he could do as he pleased because his parents and other adults would not stick to their word? In his eyes, we were weak, and he did not have to listen to us. I was absolutely devastated by the incident, but I was helpless because my boss had not followed through with the rules.

If I would have had the knowledge back then that I do now, I wouldn't have lost sleep or shed tears over the situation. I would have chosen to be happy regardless of what the others chose to do. I would have accepted the things I could not change. I could not change what the principal and the child's parent agreed upon, and I could not change that his parent only seemed to be looking at the child's fifth-grade year and not how any of it would affect his future. They were doing their best, even if I didn't agree with what they chose. Had I known then, I would not have allowed it to steal my peace and waste my time. I cannot even begin to calculate the amount of time I invested on that one family, outside the realm of my job, but the boy's parents had no interest in being partners in his education; they expected me to serve as a pawn to deliver only what they expected. If I would have had the confidence I do now, I probably would have asked that the child be placed with another teacher. If I had more confidence, I would have spoken up to his parents and the principal instead of just complaining to my family and friends about the unfairness of the situation.

This is just one example of parents wanting to shield their children from any and all discomfort or responsibility. Don't get me wrong: I have four children of my own, and I would not want them to feel pain, but I am also aware that growing pains are a necessary part of learning. My dad told me, "All people have to learn the same basic lessons. The younger you are when you learn it, the easier it is," and he couldn't have been more correct. We all have to learn to share, respect others, save, and work, among many other responsibilities in life. If we are not taught these things from a young age, we will eventually learn the hard way, whether it be getting fired, a relationship falling apart, or a parent who finally runs out of money to support you. It is much easier to learn to respect others in the elementary years than to learn in the adult years with a nasty left hook.

I often wonder where responsibility has gone. Multiple times a day, we hear someone blaming someone else, whether it be children, friends, spouses, co-workers, the media, or politicians. I remember a time in my life when I blamed my husband for my lack of happiness, and it seemed normal because those around me were doing the same thing. On the other hand, he was blaming me for his unhappiness, so it seemed logical. The greatest blessing to my life was when I began taking responsibility for everything in my life. I had to realize that *I* create my circumstances, either by an action or an omission of action, that *I* am in charge of making the choices that directly affect my life. I cannot blame anyone else for that.

Do you go to work and complain about your family, then go home and complain about your boss, co-workers, or employees? What is your responsibility in the equation?

Are you taking your responsibility or only blaming others? I have the choice to be happy in a traffic jam, a crisis, when my husband does or does not clean, or when my children refuse to listen to me. I can choose to be happy with a little or a lot. My response is my responsibility!

People live under the misconception that things are always someone else's fault, but this couldn't be farther from the truth. We make choices, and those choices come with responsibility:

- You chose to work at that company or for that person or for yourself and to continue working there.

- You chose to marry that person and to stay married to them.

- You let others or situations upset you and make you angry; no one can hurt your feelings or make you angry unless you allow them to.

Almost all situations come with warning signals, but we often choose to ignore them, to stick our heads in the sand and hope it will all go away. Just as ignorance is no defense to the law, ignorance is no defense for failing to enjoy life. There are hundreds of self-help books written by people who have walked in your shoes and have good advice to share, but you have to accept the responsibility to let them guide you. You must be willing to learn from them.

We also have a responsibility to understand others. Just as you want to be understood, so do the people around you. I have wonderful relationships because I have put time and effort into understanding others.

John, my brother, lived with my husband and I for a while, back when I didn't have the resources for understanding people like I do now. Back then, my feelings were hurt quite easily. I thought everyone was like me, so I treated people the way I wanted to be treated. I have since learned that some people are completely irritated when someone dances around an issue. John once said, "I prefer to get in trouble by Bobby. He just says, 'Don't leave the door open,' and it's over. Denise, you, on the other hand, always give me a twenty-minute lecture about why I shouldn't leave the door open." My husband and I still laugh about that to this day. I have already told my son that when he starts driving, it would be in his best interest to let his father teach him. I am aware that my ways will not be as effective as my husband's in this area, but when it comes to someone breaking his heart, I'll be there to handle that!

I am responsible for how I communicate with those around me and learning how they prefer to be treated so I can lift them up rather than tearing them down. So many of the situations I hear about could be fixed by simply taking time to understand others and to realize how they internalize things, to learn their strengths, weaknesses, fears, and personalities.

My friend owns a store, and she has learned how to prevent possible trouble with people of certain personalities. She takes extra time to go over things with some people to ensure that they understand, so problems won't be created later. She knows that she sometimes has to repeat things several times and in several different ways, and understanding that some people need this has benefitted her in her personal and business life.

Some people are huggers like me, but I have learned that this can be very uncomfortable for some people. Nowadays, if I know someone does not like such closeness, I do my best to avoid hugging them, or I apologize and say, "Sorry. I'm a hugger." I do my best to handle people with care, the kind of care they prefer, and I can only do that by understanding them.

This also holds true for different learning styles. Some people are visual learners, some like to read aloud, some read in a quiet room multiple times, some are auditory, and some are hands-on. We must give people the same respect a teacher would give a student, paying attention to the individual's needs. The benefit for you will be incredible relationships because it will show others that you care and that you can communicate effectively.

Of course you can't predict every person that you meet; in those situations, you just do your best. If someone gets angry, you may have to make some adjustments. For example, I once made a comment about a supposed weight-loss product. I did not feel that anyone within earshot needed to lose weight, and it was not an insult at all. The next day, though, I received a phone call from my friend, saying I had hurt her feelings because I'd said something about losing weight. I let my friend speak her mind, but I slept well that night, knowing I had the best intentions. I was sorry that her feelings were hurt by my words, but I had no way of predicting that she would internalize them that way. It had to do with how she viewed herself, not how

I viewed her, and I couldn't change what was in her head. I was actually proud of my BB rate that time, because in the past, I would have felt bad about it for weeks; this time, I was quickly able to realize it was a case of accepting what I could not change.

Everybody, Somebody, Anybody, and Nobody

(Author Unknown)

There was an important job to be done, and Everybody was asked to do it. Everybody was sure Somebody would do it. Anybody could have done it, but Nobody did it. Somebody got angry about that, because it was Everybody's job. Everybody thought Anybody could do it, but Nobody realized that Everybody wouldn't. It ended up that Everybody blamed Somebody, when actually Nobody asked Anybody.

CHAPTER 6

Tough Love

"What lies in our power to do, it lies in our power not to do."

~ Aristotle

Tough love, true to its name, is the hardest way to love someone, but inevitably, some people in your life will require this approach.

Since my dad was an active member of AA for about twenty-five years, I learned about enabling, but I had to go through some of my own personal experiences before I realized that I was, in fact, enabling others to continue their behavior.

You do not have to be a doormat for others, nor do you have to pay for those who are unwilling to pay or earn their own ride. However, you do need to realize that your actions or omission of actions could be allowing them to continue in those behaviors. As I said before, the responsibility is yours, and how you allow others to treat you is a choice you make.

If you have friends who complain too much, chances are it is because you are willing to listen. If you stop listening, either by leaving the situation or changing the subject every time they start to rant, they will ultimately stop complaining or keep their distance from you when they do.

If you continue to give money to your child who spends it foolishly, they will keep asking for more. As hard as it is to say no, it is a necessary part of life.

My husband and I went through those hard moments of listening to our children cry when they were forced to sleep in their own rooms. It broke our hearts, of course, but we also knew it was best for them and for us. We did not want them to be six, seven, or eight years old and sleeping in our room. We both tried to be around during the really tough starts of the training, but we had to take breaks and were often in tears because it hurt us worse than it hurt the children. It wasn't luck that our children slept in their own rooms early in life; it was tough love, and it was heartbreaking but necessary.

Just because a person says "no", that does not mean they don't love or appreciate another. I have been in direct sales for a number of years, but I have to actually applaud people for having the ability to say no. I despise pity-buying, purchases made just to avoid hurting someone's feelings. If a no hurts someone's feelings, they need to hear it a bit more often so they can toughen up and realize that it isn't always a bad thing. I expect people to say no without guilt rather than making a purchase they can't afford, don't really want, won't use, or will not be happy with later. My experiences as a salesperson allowed me to understand that every appointment would have an outcome. Either they were going to make a purchase that would help my income and provide them with something they needed, they were going to teach me something I needed to learn, or I was going to teach them something they needed to learn. I could be content with that, even if I don't know what that outcome will be. Once I understood this, I began to enjoy my job. T.I.M.E. taught me not to worry about the results but just to enjoy the ride. I have made some of the greatest lifelong friends through my business, and the mistakes I've made have only increased my BB rate in life.

Loved ones have often asked me for things, everything from money to a place to live to serving on a committee. When one asked me to lend them some money while I was in a tight spot, I decided I could work a couple of things out to make it happen. They promised to repay me in two weeks, and I made it clear that I wouldn't be able to wait any longer than that. I also assured them that I would try hard not to develop an opinion of how they chose to spend their money. I really didn't want there to be any angst or bitterness or resentment between us, nor did I want to put myself in a situation where I might exhibit that judging behavior. After I enlightened them to all of this, they declined the offer; about a month later, I learned that they had created several financial mishaps that they needed to square away, and I realized I never would have gotten my money back on time. I was thankful I'd been honest with them, that I'd exhibited tough love and chosen my words carefully. I had put the responsibility on them to do what they were promising, and they declined my offer because they knew they could not live up to that promise. Had they accepted and not paid me back on time, I would have been unable to pay my bills. T.I.M.E. had taught me to better communicate with others, and that allowed me to use the right words. There was a time in my life when I would have jumped through hoops to make their life easier, but I would have ended up mad, upset, angry, or taking jabs at them.

Another time, someone asked if we could provide them with lodging. Thankfully, we were once again smart at the start and laid some ground rules: They could stay for two weeks at no cost, but they would have to work for us in exchange for food and lodging. The one thing we did not specify was the number of hours to be worked, but we were confident enough to be honest with the individual. I enjoyed having the extra hands around to help with the kids, with doing dishes, and with outdoor projects. In my opinion, the individual needed to adjust their priorities in life, but that was not for me to decide. I could not read their mind or know their fears, weaknesses, strengths, or insecurities. All I could do was keep myself from feeling that I was giving more to the situation than I was receiving. Midway through the two weeks, I explained, "I love you enough that I will not allow you to continue to stay here if it is not helping you become your best." They looked at me strangely, and I clarified, "I love you enough to kick you out so I don't hold you back from your potential." I shared that in my past, I had loved people the wrong way and had actually caused and enabled them to linger in their bad behaviors longer by making life easier for them and carrying burdens that were not mine to carry. I told this individual, "I love you enough that I will not hurt you that way."

Tough love also exists in marriage. I allowed my husband the opportunity for a greater life when I got out of his way. I refused to allow him to control my emotions. After I took time to get in tune with what I wanted out of life, I shared it with him. I let him know that if he wanted something different, I would support him and be his friend, but I could no longer live like we were living. People wonder why our relationship is so strong today, and the simple answer is that we both made choices to learn and improve ourselves. We have both been willing to use tough love on the other when necessary. I know my husband wants only the best for me, even if my feelings tell me different sometimes. He no longer allows me to abuse him when my feelings are irrational, and that forces me to find other solutions. Just like my karate-chopping friend and her perfect physique, my husband and I were willing to sacrifice when others chose not to, and we deserve what we rightfully worked to create. If someone says to me, "It must be nice," my answer is, "Yes, it is. If you want it too, we will gladly teach you everything we know." However, what I have learned is that very few are willing to put in the work.

CHAPTER 7

No Regrets

"Life is not so much a problem to be solved as a mystery to be lived."

~ Anonymous

So many people live a defeated, average life. They are happy to eke by, and they don't even dream about more. They do not live with a true sense of peace and joy. Instead, they choose to live life as if happiness is just out of their reach. I know this because I was once one of those people, and once you have gone over that mountain, it is easy to recognize this behavior, which is typical for many of the people you come into contact with in your daily life.

The American Dream that once inspired our ancestors to achieve has been replaced by a very minimal thinking that has come to be viewed as the normal. Very few live a life they are passionate about, yet in our imaginary worlds, we crave this passion, whether from a romance movie, an inspiring story about someone else, or a co-worker who is half your age and double your looks. Many people live with a why-does-s/he-have-that-and-I-don't? attitude. There's a simple answer: Because either s/he is doing something you're not willing to do or his/her outward appearance is disguising the fact that the individual feels the same way inside as you do.

My amazing grandmother will soon be 102 years old. Most are astonished by this fact, but they are completely unaware of the implications of living a life so long. Her mind is intact, surprisingly enough, but her body is growing weaker. The reality is that every passing day brings us all a day closer to death, and she will eventually take her last breath. She is so strong and has had to overcome so many struggles throughout her life. She lost her husband early, suffered through the death of her youngest child, moved several times, and has lost friends along the way. I would like to say she has become immune to the pain of losing loved ones because she's suffered so many losses, but I know that it is not true. She still feels the pain and misses those who have gone before her, but she has no regrets. She doesn't spend time beating herself up about what she hasn't done in her life; rather, she's satisfied about what she has accomplished.

Although she is not the oldest person alive, she is very much a scholar of life. She understands the true components, has watched history repeat itself, and has learned how to continue through the pain. She accepts life for what life is and knows that she is not in control of the final breath. She lives in the moment and does not bother predicting or projecting what is not there. She is the pillar of our family, and we all hold a special place in our hearts for the dear woman. Her life is simple and always has been. One box is more than enough for Christmas. Her furnishings have been around for my entire life and then some. She has not been lured by the next, newest, latest, or greatest; rather, she loves to make memories related to the three F's—faith, family, and friends. If it doesn't rank in those areas, you can almost bet it doesn't rank on her list of important things in life.

Grandma has lived a full life, every minute full of memories—the kind of memories that replay in the heart during the quiet moments, those that draw a smile when no one is around, those that bring comfort and warmth. She is not cluttered with stuff because she knows stuff is overrated.

She is so often filled with words of praise for accomplishments, boasting about her family and what they are doing, actually using words to tell us she is proud of us. At times when I have been down about finances or other challenges in life, Grandma has reminded me how proud she is of me for choosing to stay home with my kids, and that makes all the difference.

My children are still young and have only had the opportunity to visit her from two to five times, as she lives states away. Nevertheless, because of who she is and how she talks to them, they speak about her at least once a week. The twins are ninety-nine years younger than she, but they know who she is and speak about her. She has kept our family connected through the years, even while we occupied seven different states.

This past September, it was time to take a road trip to move my grandma. When I spoke to my dad, he told me he would drive to Kansas and gave me the approximate dates. He didn't ask me if I wanted to go, but I knew I would be in that car with him, no matter what it took. It was, after all, an opportunity to see my grandma, and it would cost me nothing but time.

The morning we were supposed to leave, I had no plans of taking any of my four children on the seventeen-hour trip, but as I was on my way out the door, my oldest daughter said, "I want to go with you." Even though it wasn't part of the plan and I hadn't packed a thing for her, within fifteen minutes, she was in the car, ready for her trip with Grandpa Karl and Mom. Her little brother and sister would stay at home, and her older brother couldn't go because of school. It was the trip of a lifetime for her, and she talks about it all the time. We ran out of gas in Kentucky, she stayed at a hotel with an indoor pool, she played Go Fish with Great Grandma Lois, she made two new friends named Beth and Sandy, she got to take a real shower instead of a bath, she had her mother and grandpa all to herself, and she was the absolute princess of the trip, with Great Grandma Lois for a queen and Grandpa Karl for a king.

The adjustments to my grandma's living situation made the end of our time with her seem even closer. I will never forget the lesson my dad shared in that burgundy Suburban: "I told my mama long ago everything I need to say. Now, every time I get to see her or talk to her, it is icing on the cake."

Four months later, my dad died.

The man who shares my daughter's name left her life. Because she'd just turned four, her memory of him is limited, but our trip is imprinted on her heart. She lights up when she asks, "Remember when we went to Kansas with Grandpa Karl, and we ran out of gas?" Karlee will forever carry with her that treasured memory. I can't give my kids any more time with my dad because the time ran out, but while the clock was still ticking, I made choices that gave them all I could of him.

He passed on at the young age of sixty-six, and it came as quite a shock to his three older brothers and his mom. It was hard for me as well, but I quickly found peace, serenity, and acceptance of my best friend's death because I had no regrets. I had lunch with my dad often, whenever I was in his town, and we did many projects together. I often asked his advice, and during the last year of his life, we made two roundtrips together, one about twenty-two hours and the other about thirty-four, all those hours just talking and sharing. I had long ago told my dad everything I needed to say and all the rest was icing on the cake! I did not miss opportunities to make real memories with my father, all of them centered on faith, family, and friends.

I so often hear excuses as to why people are not moving forward. Many claim they are waiting, claiming they'll make changes when:

- The kids go to school
- The kids get out of school
- Summer comes
- Winter comes

- The holidays are over

- The weight is lost or gained

- They get married or divorced

- They make more or less money

People are waiting their lives away, planning to enjoy it later, but the greatest opportunities come at the most inopportune times. You must be willing to make a move when those opportunities come knocking, because if you wait, that chance might not be available for long.

My husband offered to train a narcotics detection dog for another individual. Thanks to word-of-mouth, his reputation grew, and within a few months, several people were asking for his help in this field. He did what he could on the side, so when his full-time employment ended, he was already in a position to pick up and move forward with the dogs. Had he not taken those small steps when they presented themselves, he would have not been prepared when the sudden job loss came.

We expect everyone to move naturally through all of life's stages: walk, talk, hear, go to school, date, get married, go to college, have a career, and have children and grandchildren. When our children do not follow this pattern, we grow antsy, concerned, and worried and try to push it on them. The most important thing in life is not the path it takes; the most important thing is that while we are walking through, we focus on the guiding principles: T.I.M.E., time, doing our best, taking responsibility, and exercising tough love. Only then can we be confident and passionate about living a life worth living, and only then can we pass it on!

Make a vow today to begin living with no regrets! Walk through unknown doors when they open; if you wait until you are certain of the outcome, you will surely miss what is waiting for you on that path. Just jump in the car and take the trip, for you never know where it will lead or what you'll see along the way.

Conclusion

My hope is that you have found something within these pages that will propel you to your next level, that you will begin to see your life as an opportunity to make a difference in someone else's. We all run out of time, so make the most out of what is given to you. Face your fears, take risks, be challenged, and, most of all, love all who cross your path.

Don't look for the biggest house or the best car...Strive to be the best that you can be!

Sincerely,

Denise Mercer Blackwell

About the Author

"Seek the good in every situation and in every person."

~Denise Mercer Blackwell

Denise Mercer Blackwell was raised in Michigan. After finishing college there, she moved to North Carolina in search of warmer weather and on a personal quest to discover for herself if God was, in fact, real. She discovered the truths she'd gone looking for, and along the way, she also learned that there is more to life than just breathing and running in circles like a hamster on a wheel. She has experienced many things in life, but through all the twists and turns, mistakes and lessons, she has gotten back up and kept moving forward, always believing that the best is yet to come.

www.ingramcontent.com/pod-product-compliance
Lightning Source LLC
Chambersburg PA
CBHW051833040426
42447CB00006B/510